A Note to Parents

D0282268

DK READERS is a compelling pro
readers, designed in conjunction w
experts, including Dr. Linda Gambrell, Distin
Professor of Education at Clemson University. Dr. Gambrell has served as President of the National Reading Conference, the College Reading Association, and the International Reading Association.

Beautiful illustrations and superb full-color photographs combine with engaging, easy-to-read stories to offer a fresh approach to each subject in the series. Each DK READER is guaranteed to capture a child's interest while developing his or her reading skills, general knowledge, and love of reading.

The five levels of DK READERS are aimed at different reading abilities, enabling you to choose the books that are exactly right for your child:

Pre-level 1: Learning to read
Level 1: Beginning to read
Level 2: Beginning to read alone
Level 3: Reading alone
Level 4: Proficient readers

The "normal" age at which a child begins to read can be anywhere from three to eight years old. Adult participation through the lower levels is very helpful for providing encouragement, discussing storylines, and sounding out unfamiliar words.

No matter which level you select, you can be sure that you are helping your child learn to read, then read to learn!

LONDON, NEW YORK, MUNICH,
MELBOURNE, AND DELHI

Written by Fiona Lock

Series Editor Deborah Lock
U.S. Editor John Searcy
Project Art Editor Mary Sandberg
Production Editor Siu Yin Chan
Production Claire Pearson
Jacket Designer Mary Sandberg

Reading Consultant
Linda Gambrell, Ph.D.

First American Edition, 2009
12 13 10 9 8 7
Published in the United States by DK Publishing
375 Hudson Street, New York, New York 10014
011-DD503-Mar/2009
Copyright © 2009 Dorling Kindersley Limited

All rights reserved under International and Pan-American Copyright Conventions. No part of this publication may be reproduced, stored in a retrieval system, or transmitted in an form or by any means, electronic, mechanical, photocopying, recording, or otherwise, without the prior written permission of the copyright owner.
Published in Great Britain by Dorling Kindersley Limited

DK books are available at special discounts when purchased in bulk for sales promotions, premiums, fund-raising, or educational use.
For details, contact:
DK Publishing Special Markets
375 Hudson Street
New York, New York 10014
SpecialSales@dk.com

A catalog record for this book
is available from the Library of Congress
ISBN: 978-0-7566-4295-2 (Paperback)
ISBN: 978-0-7566-4294-5 (Hardcover)

Color reproduction by Colourscan, Singapore
Printed and bound in China by L Rex Printing Co., Ltd.

The publisher would like to thank Elizabeth Bartlett as equestrian consultant.
The publisher would also like to thank the following for their kind permission to reproduce their photographs:
a=above; b=below; c=center; l=left; r=right; t=top
Alamy Images: Tim Graham 20-21; Peter Llewellyn 17c; Lourens Smak 15tr. **Corbis:** Walter Bieri / EPA 22t; Christopher Cormack 27t; Ariel Skelley 7t. **DK Images:** Mr. and Mrs. Dimmock 8br, 9bc; John Goddard Fenwick and Lyn Moran 22bl; Haras National de Compiegne, France 19bc; Miss. H Houlden 7bl, 7fbr; Stephen Oliver 6c, 16br, 17bc, 21br, 21fbl; Stephen Oliver / Courtesy of Sally Chaplin 29br, 29fbl; Darwin Olsen, Kentucky Horse Park, USA 8bl, 9bl, 9fbr; Pegasus Stables, Newmarket 24br, 25bl. **FLPA:** Gerard Lacz 18-19, 30bl. **Getty Images:** Gallo Images / Travel Ink 4-5. **Masterfile:** R. Ian Lloyd 28-29. **Photolibrary:** Creatas 12-13. **Shutterstock:** Condor 36 31br; Dennis Donohue 24-25; Kondrashov MIkhail Evgenevich 16t. **Still Pictures:** Biosphoto / Klein J.-L. & Hubert M.-L. 14-15. **SuperStock:** Age Fotostock 30-31.
Jacket images *Front:* **Getty Images:** National Geographic / Ralph Lee Hopkins.
All other images © Dorling Kindersley
For further information see: www.dkimages.com

Discover more at

www.dk.com

Contents

4 Stable yard
6 Ponies
8 Brown horses
10 Palomino ponies
12 Chestnut horses
14 Foals
16 Black horses
18 Gray ponies
20 Bay horses
22 Dancing horses
24 Racehorses
26 Polo ponies
28 Ranch horses
30 Wild horses
32 Glossary

DK READERS

Ponies and Horses

DK Publishing

Welcome to
the stable yard.
The horses are
eating and drinking.

hay

The pony has to be brushed and washed.

ponies

brown horses

The brown horse
has horseshoes
fitted to its hooves.

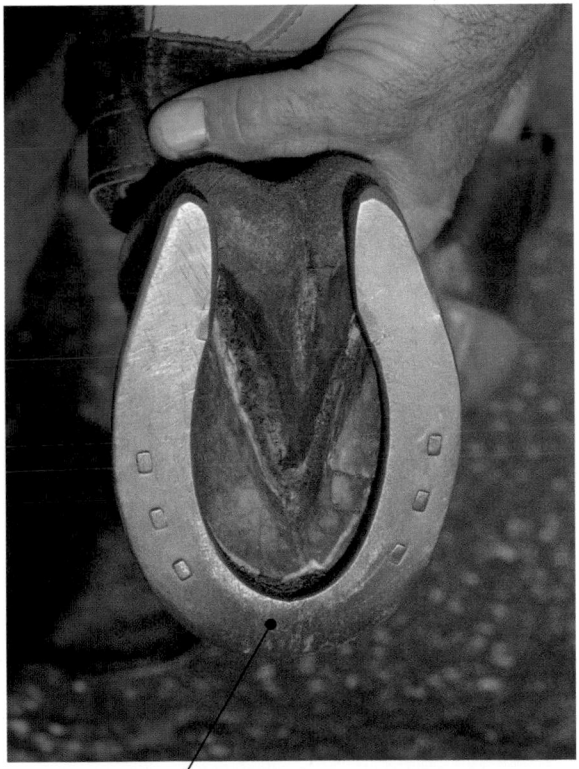

The rider puts a saddle on the palomino [pal-uh-MEE-no] pony.

palomino ponies

The chestnut horses go for a walk. The riders wear riding hats.
chestnut horses

riding hat
bridle

The horse and its foal graze in the field.

foals

foal

black horses

People watch
the black horses at
the horse show.

The rider tells
the gray pony to trot
and then to canter.
gray ponies

rider

The bay horse jumps over the fence.
fence
bay horses

dancing horses

The dancing horses jump and leap.

racehorses

The racehorses race around the track. Who will win?

polo stick
polo ponies

The polo ponies
run up and down
the polo field.

Cowboys ride ranch horses to round up the cattle.

ranch horses

cowboy
cattle

The wild horses gallop across a river.

Can you gallop

like a horse?

Glossary

Brush a tool for brushing the hair of a horse

Fence a row of bars for a horse to jump over

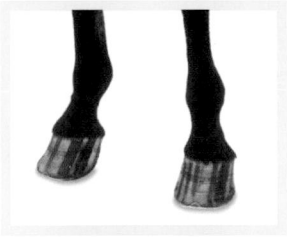

Hooves the feet of a horse

Riding hat a hard hat that a horse rider wears

Saddle a seat for a rider that is tied onto a horse's back